Leckie
the education publisher
for Scotland

Primary Maths
for Scotland

T0337209

2nd Level Maths

2A

Practice Workbook 2

© 2024 Leckie

001/12092024

10 9 8 7 6 5 4 3 2 1

ISBN 9780008680343

Published by
Leckie
An imprint of HarperCollins Publishers
Westerhill Road, Bishopbriggs, Glasgow, G64 2QT

T: 0844 576 8126 F: 0844 576 8131
leckiescotland@harpercollins.co.uk www.leckiescotland.co.uk

HarperCollins Publishers
Macken House, 39/40 Mayor Street Upper, Dublin 1, D01 C9W8, Ireland

Publisher: Fiona McGlade

Special thanks
Project editor: Peter Dennis
Layout: Jouve
Proofreader: Julianna Dunn

A CIP Catalogue record for this book is available from the British Library.

Acknowledgements
Images © Shutterstock.com

Printed in the UK by Martins the Printers

This book contains FSC™ certified paper and other controlled sources to ensure responsible forest management.

For more information visit: www.harpercollins.co.uk/green

Contents

Answers

Check your answers to this workbook online: https://collins.co.uk/pages/scottish-primary-maths

6.1 Comparing fractions

1 Label the coloured parts of the fraction bars.

one eighth   one tenth   one quarter   one twelfth

a)

b)

c)

d)

2 a) Label the coloured parts of the bar models.

half   eighth   fifth   tenth

sixth   twelfth   quarter

i)

ii)

iii)

iv)

v)

vi)

vii)

b) Circle **True** or **False** for each of these statements. If **False**, correct the statement so it is true.

i) One third is larger than one half.   True   False

ii) One half is not the same size as two quarters.   True   False

iii) Four of the bar models show equivalent fractions.   True   False

iv) Five tenths is larger than one third but smaller than four eighths. True   False

★ Challenge

Write your own true or false statements comparing the following fractions:

a) one half and two thirds   True   False

b) three quarters and four eighths   True   False

c) five tenths and eight twelfths   True   False

1 Finlay and his dad share a bar of chocolate.

a) Which portion can Finlay choose so that he gets exactly half? Insert a ✓ beside the portions that Finlay could choose.

b) Name the fraction shown by each darker portion of chocolate. One has been done for you.

i)
✓

one half

ii)

iii)

iv)

v)

vi)

vii)

viii)

ix)

xv)

2

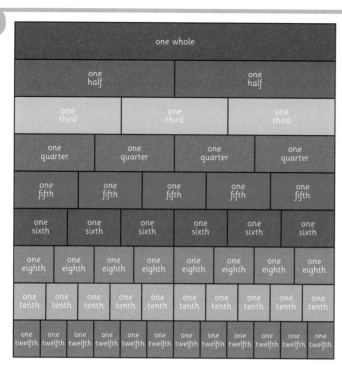

a) Amman is to get two thirds of a chocolate bar. Identify and name a fraction that is equivalent to two thirds.

b) Nuria is to get one quarter of a chocolate bar. Identify and name the fractions that are equivalent to one quarter.

⭐ **Challenge**

Match the fractions on the left, to the written description and the equivalent fraction on the right.

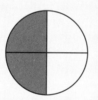

four sixths

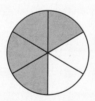

six eighths

two quarters

three twelfths

1 Isla is investigating what happens when thirds are split into two parts, three parts and six parts. Help her by naming each of these fractions and writing fractions that are equal to one third. The first one has been done for you.

_____thirds_____   _____   _____   _____

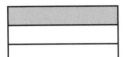 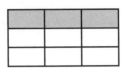 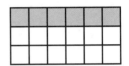

____one third____ = _____ = _____ = _____

2 Colour to match the equivalent fractions below. You will need yellow, blue, red, pink and green coloured pencils.

	four sixteenths	one half		

two quarters	six tenths	seventy-five hundredths	fifty hundreds	twenty thirtieths

twenty-five hundredths			one quarter	two thirds

3 Nuria has made some statements about fractions. Shade the boxes to create the equivalent fractions to prove she is correct.

a) Two thirds is equal to four sixths.

 =

b) Three quarters is equal to fifteen twentieths.

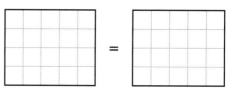

c) Four fifths is equal to eight tenths.

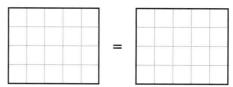

⭐ Challenge

Use the grids below to create equivalent fractions. One has been done for you.
Draw fractions equivalent to:

a) one half

b) two fifths

c) one third

d) six eighths

e) eight tenths

6.4 Simplifying fractions

1 Draw a line to match each red fraction to the blue simplified version.

a)

two sixths

one quarter

b)

six sixteenths

two fifths

c)

three twelfths

one third

d)

four tenths

three eighths

2 Write what each of these fractions are. Colour the equivalent simplified fraction and write what the fraction is. The first one has been started for you.

a) =

four eighths

_____

b) =

_____

_____

c) =

_____

_____

d) =

_____

_____

3 Complete the bar models to show how the following fractions can be simplified. Write which fractions you have created. The first one has been done for you.

_____ two quarters _____ = _____ one half _____

a) =

_____ sixths _____   _____

b) =

_____ tenths _____   _____

c) =

_____ twelfths _____   _____

d) =

_____ eighths _____   _____

★ **Challenge**

Fill in the answer boxes to create fractions that cannot be simplified and are in their simplest form.

a) [   ] twentieths   b) [   ] twenty-fourths

c) [   ] fifteenths   d) [   ] eighteenths

6.5 Writing decimal equivalents to tenths

1 Write the amount coloured on each diagram as a fraction and a decimal fraction. The first one has been done for you.

a)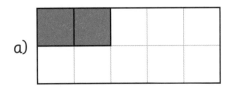

two tenths = 0·2

b)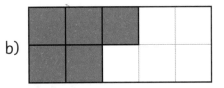

c)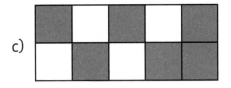

d)

2 Convert these fractions to decimal fractions.

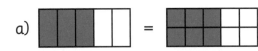

a) = three fifths = | = |

b) = | = | = |

c) = | = | = |

d) = | = | = |

e) = | = | = |

3 Write the following amounts in three different ways. The first one has been done for you.

a) 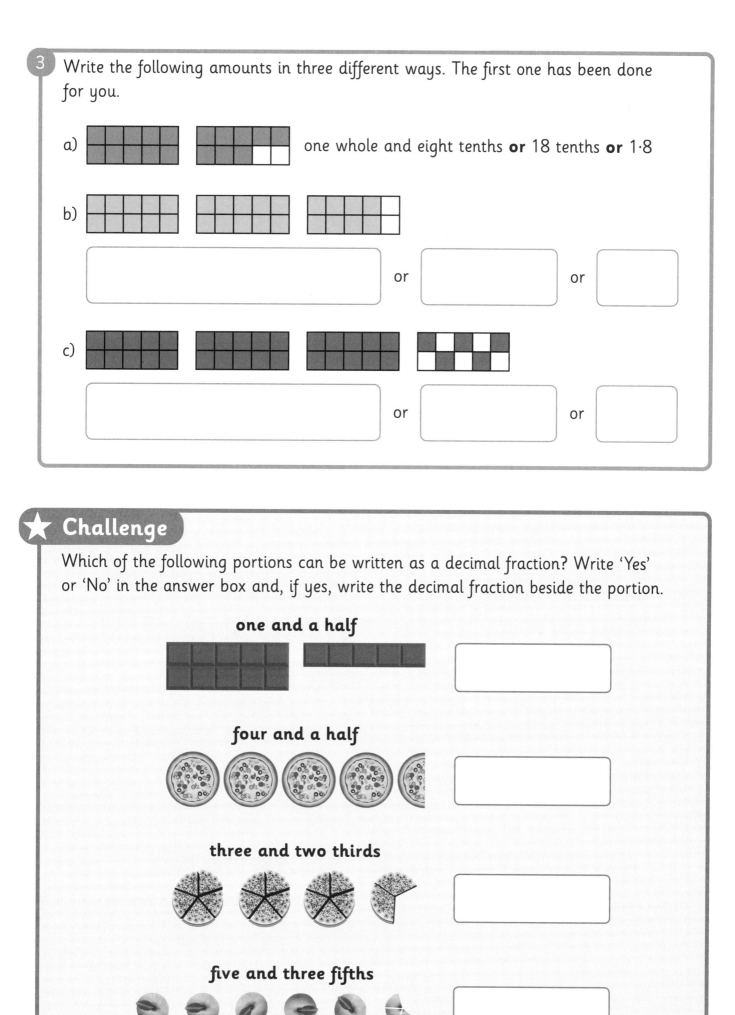 one whole and eight tenths **or** 18 tenths **or** 1·8

b)

	or		or	

c)

	or		or	

⭐ **Challenge**

Which of the following portions can be written as a decimal fraction? Write 'Yes' or 'No' in the answer box and, if yes, write the decimal fraction beside the portion.

one and a half

four and a half

three and two thirds

five and three fifths

6.6 Comparing numbers with one decimal place

1 Write a statement using decimal numbers to compare each of the bar models below. The first one has been done for you.

a)

0·4 is smaller than 0·6

b)

c)

d)

2 a) Use the number line below and write the numbers in the correct positions.

| 3·5 | 2·2 | 2 | 1·8 | 2·5 | 3 | 1·6 | 2·8 | 3·1 | 2·3 |

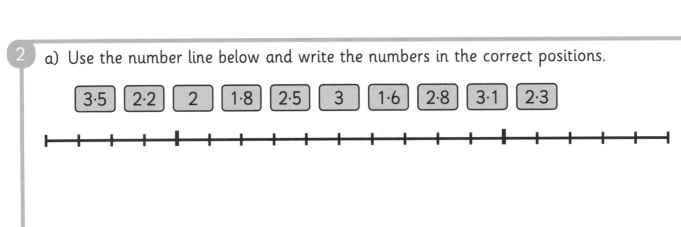

b) Write 5 statements using these numbers.

2·5 is larger than 1·8	

3. Nine Gentoo penguins from Edinburgh Zoo are being weighed. Write their names in the correct order from the lightest to the heaviest penguin.

Kevin 8·1 kg	Snowflake 6·9 kg	Chad 5 kg	Brenda 5·5 kg	Bailey 7·5 kg

Gary 6·7 kg	Mary 4·5 kg	Mark 7·8 kg	Helen 6 kg

a) Write these numbers in the correct section of the Venn Diagram.

| 10·4 | 2·3 | 3·4 | 2·8 | 6·9 | 2·1 | 3·6 | 20·4 |

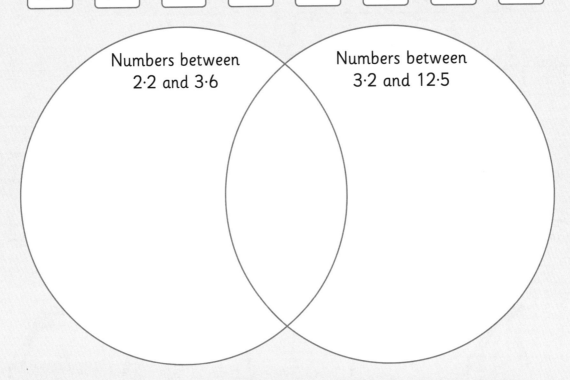

Numbers between 2·2 and 3·6

Numbers between 3·2 and 12·5

b) Write numbers on the blank cards that will fit **on** and **outside** the Venn Diagram.

Numbers between 2·2 and 3·6

Numbers between 3·2 and 12·5

6.7 Calculating a simple fraction of a value

1 Use the bar models to work out the following:

a) two thirds of 15

15

b) three quarters of 28

28

c) four fifths of 20

20

d) three tenths of 30.

30

2 Complete the bar model to show how you could work out the following:

a) three quarters of 32

b) two fifths of 25

c) three sevenths of 14

[   ]

d) five sixths of 24

[   ]

e) five eighths of 40

[   ]

f) three tenths of 40

[   ]

3 Draw a bar model to solve each of the following problems.

a) Edinburgh Zoo has lots of different species of penguins. There are 50 Rockhopper penguins at the zoo. Nine tenths of them are adults.

How many adult Rockhoppers are there?

b) Five ninths of the 72 Gentoo penguins at the zoo are female.

How many are female?

c) Edinburgh Zoo has a Penguin Parade every lunchtime where penguins can go for a walk outside their enclosure if they want to. Three eighths of the penguins who are outside take part in it. There are 32 penguins outside. How many take part?

Write and solve word problems represented by the bar models below.

a)
27

b)
35

c)
32

d)
60

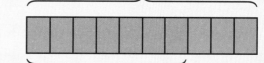

7.1 Writing amounts using decimal notation

1 Complete the following table. The first one has been done for you.

Amount in Words	Amount in p	Amount in £
Five pounds and twenty three pence	523p	£5·23
	723p	
		£7·03
Ninety-two pence		
	9276p	
		£93·78

2 Write the following amounts using decimal notation. The first one has been done for you.

a) 345p = **£3·45**

b) Three pounds and sixty-five pence =

c) 765p =

d) Fifteen pounds and seventy-five pence =

e) 1505p =

f) 65p =

3 Write the total amount using decimal notation.

a) Two hundred and two 1p pieces = £

b) Eight £10 notes = £

c) Eight £5 notes = £

d) Fifteen 5p pieces = £

e) Seven 10p pieces = £

f) Eight 20p pieces = £

4 a) Finlay saved £2 every week for seven weeks. How much money did he save? Write this in decimal notation.

b) He wants to buy a book for £9·50 and a magazine for £5·50. What is the total in decimal notation?

c) Does he have enough money? If not, how much more does Finlay need?

d) Nuria saved £21 over 6 weeks. She saved the same amount each week. How much did she save each week? Write this in decimal notation.

★ Challenge

Different currencies are used in different countries in the world. Sometimes the same word, such as 'dollar' is used but the country's name is added to the beginning of it.

Complete the table using these clues.

- £10·00 in USD is two dollars and sixty-seven cents more than 10·00.
- £10·00 in CAD starts with seventeen and has two 1s in the cents places.
- £10·00 in NZD is double plus forty-five cents.
- The HKD is eighty-seven cents less than $100.

Currency	Conversion	Amount in Words
British Pound (GBP)	£10·00	Ten pounds
US Dollar (USD)		
Canadian Dollar (CAD)		
Australian Dollar (AUD)		Nineteen dollars and thirty-two cents
New Zealand Dollar (NZD)		
Hong Kong Dollar (HKD)		

1 Isla wants to buy a new bike that costs £145. She has already saved £83 from her birthday money.

a) How much more does she need to save?

b) If Isla gets £10 a week for walking her neighbour's dog after school, how many weeks will she need to save before she can afford the bike she wants?

2 Nuria needs to replace some items in her football kit for training next season. She has a budget of £75.

Football boots
New style
£70

Football boots
On sale
£42

Football boots
Second hand, used once
£21

Tracksuit
New style
£40

Tracksuit
On sale
£33

Tracksuit
Second hand,
never used
£10

Long-sleeved top
New
£23

Long-sleeved top
On sale
£11

Long-sleeved top
Second hand,
never used
£6

Shin guards
New
£18

Shin guards
On sale
£13

Socks
On offer
£9

a) What is the greatest number of items Nuria can buy for £75?

b) How can Nuria buy boots, a tracksuit, a long-sleeved top, shin guards and socks and have the most amount of money left over?

c) i) What do you think are the most important items for Nuria to replace? Why?

ii) Should she buy them new, on sale or second hand? Why?

3 Finlay's dad works five days a week and has budgeted £50 a week to pay for his journey to and from work. He takes the bus to the station and then catches the train to work.

The bus fare is £1·80 for a single ticket. The train fare is £6·40 for a return ticket.

a) How much does Finlay's dad spend on fares in a week?

b) How much money from his £50 budget will be left each week?

c) How much would Finlay's dad save if he cycled to the train station 3 days every week?

If you have a calculator, you are allowed to use it.

Amman is planning a trip to an outdoor adventure park for his birthday. His parents have said he can spend £100 to spend on him and his friends and it is up to him how many friends he invites.

Amman wants everyone to be able to play outdoors, have lunch, a drink and an ice-cream.

Indoor and Outdoor
Ticket – £14·35

Outdoor Adventure
Ticket – £10·00

Lunch Box – £5·95

Small Drink – £1·70

Medium Drink – £1·90

Large Drink – £2·10

One-Scoop Tub – £1·90

Two-Scoop Tub – £2·20

a) What is the maximum number of friends he can bring?

b) What is the most they can each get for lunch? How much will it cost?

c) How many friends can Amman bring if he wants to play inside **and** outside, and have the largest drinks and ice-creams? How much will he have left over?

7.3 Saving money

1

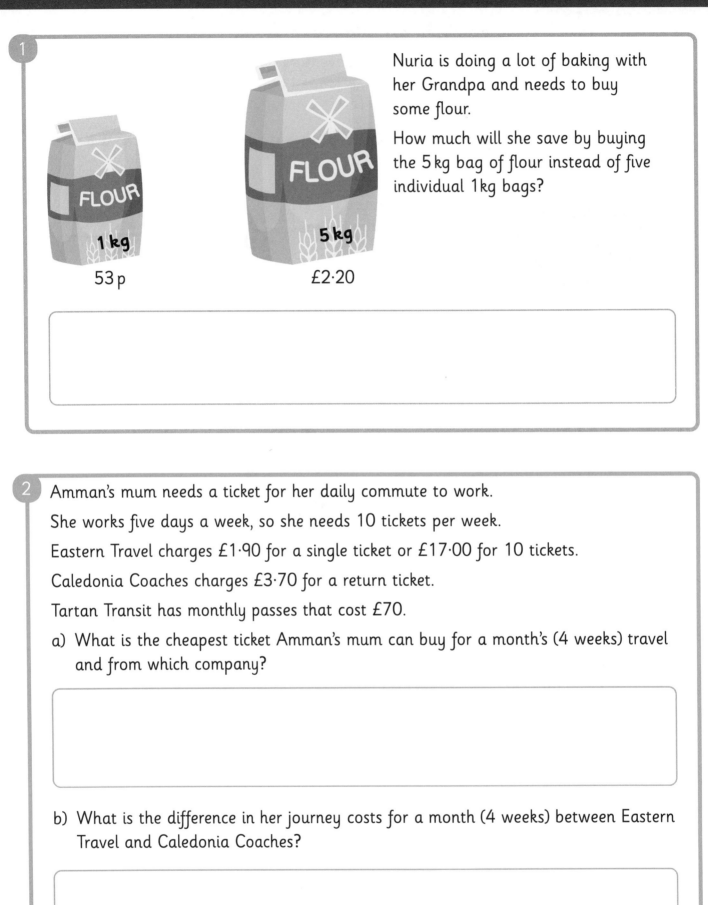

FLOUR

1 kg

53 p

FLOUR

5 kg

£2·20

Nuria is doing a lot of baking with her Grandpa and needs to buy some flour.

How much will she save by buying the 5 kg bag of flour instead of five individual 1kg bags?

2 Amman's mum needs a ticket for her daily commute to work.

She works five days a week, so she needs 10 tickets per week.

Eastern Travel charges £1·90 for a single ticket or £17·00 for 10 tickets.

Caledonia Coaches charges £3·70 for a return ticket.

Tartan Transit has monthly passes that cost £70.

a) What is the cheapest ticket Amman's mum can buy for a month's (4 weeks) travel and from which company?

b) What is the difference in her journey costs for a month (4 weeks) between Eastern Travel and Caledonia Coaches?

c) Would a monthly pass for Tartan Transit be the best value if Amman's mum was off on holiday for a week? Why?

3 Finlay's family are planning a trip for seven days during the school holidays. There will be two adults and two children. There aren't sure where they would like to go!

- A train to Inverness will cost them £185. The hotel they like will be £1450 for the family to stay together. A Family Easy-Rider bus pass for unlimited travel around Inverness and the area will be £50 for the week.
- Flights to Marseille will cost £65 per person. The villa costs £1120 and car hire will be an extra £30 per day.
- Flights to Malaga and the car hire for the week is £470. A beach-front apartment costs £1300.

a) What is the least amount Finlay's family could pay for a trip?

b) What is the most Finlay's family could pay?

c) How much will they save between the most expensive and least expensive options?

Working

Isla's dad always does the weekly shop and is willing to shop around to get the lowest prices.

CostLo	**Superstore**	**Fresh Fare**
Baked beans (pack of 6 tins) £5·25	Baked beans (pack of 6 tins) £4·25 (with discount)	Baked beans (1 can) 42 p
1 litre of milk £1·20	2 litres of milk £1·45	2 litres of milk £1·55
Chopped tomatoes 42 p	Chopped tomatoes 35 p	Chopped tomatoes 43 p
500 g minced beef £5·25	500 g minced beef £4·90	500 g minced beef £5·10

a) If Isla's dad needs to buy milk, chopped tomatoes, beans and minced beef, what is the cheapest he can buy them for?

b) Which products should Isla's dad be buying from each shop?

CostLo –

Superstore –

Fresh Fare –

c) How much would Isla's dad spend if he bought the most expensive items?

d) How much did he save by *not* doing this?

7.4 Profit and loss

1 Nuria sold 15 packs of stickers at the school fair. She bought each pack for £1 and sold them for £2. How much profit did she make?

2 Finlay's stall at the school fair was selling second-hand books. They received donations from pupils but also bought some from the local bookshop for £20. At the end of the school fair, they had £87 in their money box. How much profit did Finlay's stall make?

3 Amman was in charge of the Cake and Candy stall at the school fair. Amman's class did all the baking themselves. They spent £30 on ingredients and made £126 profit. How much was in their money box at the end of the fair?

4 When Amman's class were making tablet for the Cake and Candy stall, the ingredients for one tray of tablet cost £3·60. If they were able to make 12 bags of tablet from one tray, what is the minimum they had to sell each bag for to make a profit?

5 a) Isla and her friends were running the Tombola at the school fair. They made £110 profit and had £165 in their money box at the end of the fair. How much did they spend on items for the Tombola?

b) The Tombola stall sold 50 tickets on the day of the School Fair. How much profit was made on each ticket sold?

Nuria, Finlay, Amman and Isla made Christmas cards to sell at the school fair.

A pack of 20 blank cards & envelopes cost £2.

A pack of 100 Christmas shapes cost £5.

A pack of 100 tissue paper squares cost £1.

A pack of 50 Christmas greetings stickers cost £2.

a) How much did it cost to make 100 cards?

b) How much did it cost to make one card?

c) The four friends want to make at least 50p profit on each card they sell.
What is the minimum they must sell each Christmas card for?

1 Write the time shown in words. The first one has been done for you.

a) **4:21** Twenty one minutes past four

b) **4:29**

c) **4:51**

d) **12:41**

e)

f)

g)

h)

2 Draw the hands on the clock faces to show the times given.

a) Nineteen minutes past 6

b) Nineteen minutes to 7

c) Twenty-nine minutes past 10

d) Nine minutes to 11

3 Write the time shown. Remember to include the time of day: morning, afternoon or evening.

a) 6:44 PM

b) 8:34 AM

c) 2:36 PM

d) 3:57 AM

★ **Challenge**

Write six events into the Carrol Diagram with the time it starts, for example: **Dance Practice - 5:45 pm**. There should be at least one event in each section of the Carroll Diagram. Once you have written six events, show the times as digital and analogue on the clock faces.

	to	past
A.M.		
P.M.		

8.2 Converting between 12-h and 24-h time

1 Convert the following 12-hour times to 24-hour times.

a) 6:15 pm

b) 7:15 am

c) 2:24 pm

d) 2:56 am

e) 9:17 am

f) 10:17 pm

g) 12:00 pm

h) 12:00 am

2 Convert the following 24-hour times to 12-hour times.

a) 0430

b) 1642

c) 0202

d) 1002

e) 0001

f) 1202

g) 2357

h) 2007

3 Match the 12-hour and 24-hour digital and analogue times.

 Twenty minutes past 8

 Twenty minutes to 8

Five minutes to 4 Twenty minutes to 7

4 Write each of these times in 12-hour and 24-hour times.

a) `7:42` AM _____

b) 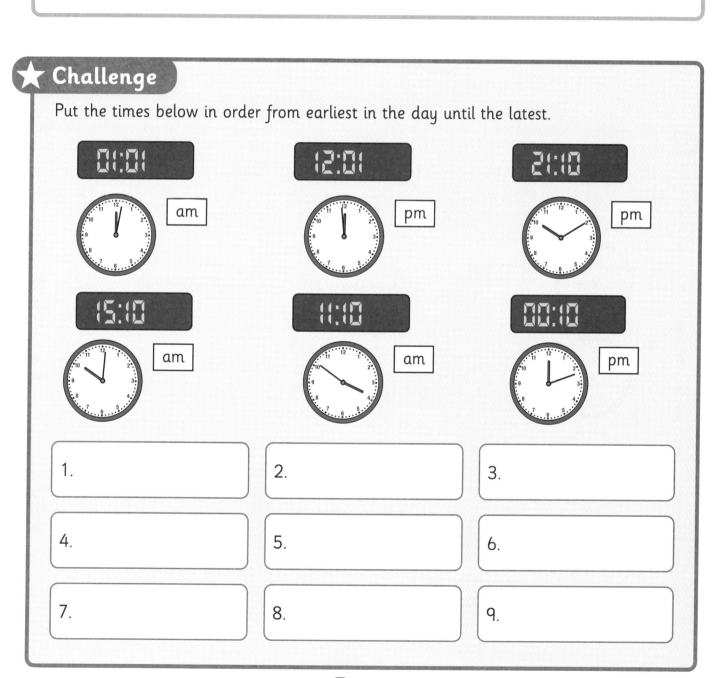 am _____

c) `11:42` PM _____

d) pm _____

e) `11:04` AM _____

f) pm _____

★ **Challenge**

Put the times below in order from earliest in the day until the latest.

`01:01`   am

`12:01`   pm

`21:10`   pm

`15:10`   am

`11:10`   am

`00:10`   pm

1. _____

2. _____

3. _____

4. _____

5. _____

6. _____

7. _____

8. _____

9. _____

35

1 Colour to sort the times into two groups. Colour the quarter to and quarter past times blue, and the half past and o'clock times red.

06:45

13:15

09:00

08:45

20:30

15:45

2 Complete the table. You may need to draw hands on the clock face and write 'am' or 'pm', write the digital time or write the time in words. One has been done for you.

	Analogue	Digital	Words
	PM	15:15	Quarter past three in the afternoon
a)		21:45	
b)		:	Twelve o'clock at night
c)	AM	:	

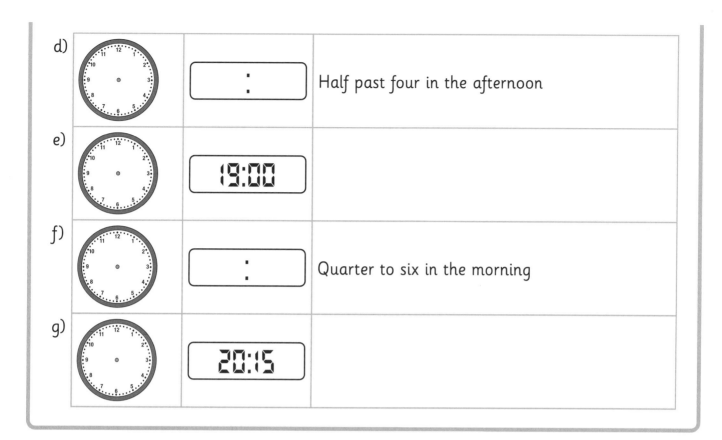

d)	`[ : ]`	Half past four in the afternoon
e)	`19:00`	
f)	`[ : ]`	Quarter to six in the morning
g)	`20:15`	

Record your answers to the questions below in three ways – digital, analogue and word form.

a) Nuria wants to catch the train in half an hour. It is quarter past eleven in the morning now. What time does the train leave?

b) Finlay's basketball practice lasts for three quarters of an hour. If practice starts at 3:45 pm, what time will it finish?

c) Amman and Isla are working on a school project together. It takes half an hour for Amman to walk to Isla's house so they can finish the project. Amman has said to Isla he will be there by 1800. What time does Amman have to leave his house?

8.4 Calculating time intervals or durations

1 Complete the timeline and work out the total time interval from start to finish.

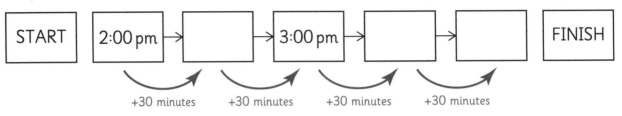

| START | 2:00 pm | | 3:00 pm | | | FINISH |

+30 minutes   +30 minutes   +30 minutes   +30 minutes

Total time interval:

2 Using the information from the train timetable, answer the questions below.

Glasgow Queen Street	0920	0950	1020
Bishopbriggs	0925	0955	1025
Lenzie	0930	1000	1030
Croy	0935	1005	1035
Larbert	0945	1015	1045
Stirling	0955	1025	1055
	1000	1030	1100
Bridge of Allan	1005	1035	1105
Dunblane	1010	1040	1110

a) Isla's mum needs to travel from Glasgow Queen Street to Dunblane. How long is her journey?

b) She arrives at Glasgow Queen Street at 9·30 am. How long does she need to wait for the train?

c) A colleague of Isla's mum joins her on the train at Lenzie. It takes her 20 minutes to walk to the station and buy a ticket. What is the latest time she has to leave her house?

3 Calculate the following time intervals using the 'chunking' method. Write the time durations you have used under the arrows.

a)
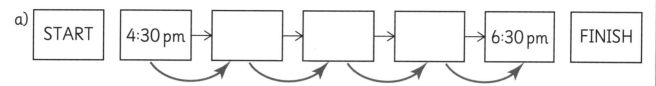

| START | 4:30 pm | → | → | → | 6:30 pm | FINISH |

b)
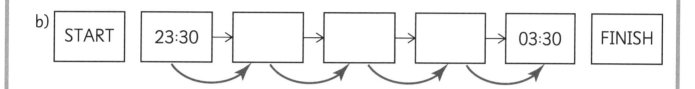

| START | 23:30 | → | → | → | 03:30 | FINISH |

c)
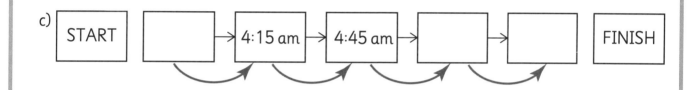

| START | | 4:15 am | 4:45 am | → | | FINISH |

★ Challenge

Isla is flying to Calgary in Canada with her mum. They leave their house at 8 am and arrive at the airport at 9 am. The flight leaves at 11:30 am and lands in Calgary at 12:45 pm local time. Calgary is 7 hours behind UK time.

How long is their total journey time?

8.5 Speed, time and distance calculations

Use the formula **Distance = Speed × Time** to calculate the distance travelled in the following questions.

1

a) Nuria cycled at 8 mph for three hours. How far did she cycle?

b) Nuria's dad can cycle 10 mph faster than Nuria. How far can he travel in three hours?

c) Nuria's mum prefers walking the dog and jogging to cycling. She charted her exercise over a week. She jogged at 10 mph for four hours and walked at 5 mph for three hours. What distance did Nuria's mum cover over the week?

2 Calculate the distance travelled in the table below.

Speed (S)	Time (T)	Distance (D)
25 mph	3 hours	
50 mph	8 hours	
120 mph	4 hours	
40 mph	5 hours	

Working

3 The overnight sleeper train left Edinburgh at 2330 and arrived in London at 0730. It travelled at an average of 50 mph.

a) How long did the journey take?

b) How many miles did the train travel?

Nuria and Isla competed in the Coast-to-Coast challenge, running, cycling and kayaking from Nairn to Loch Leven, Ballachulish over a weekend. This table shows the route, the times, how they travelled and their average speed.

SATURDAY	Time	Method of transport	Average speed
Leave Nairn	6:30 am	Trail Running	4 mph
Leave Cawdor Castle	8:00 am	Cycling	8 mph
Arrive Fort Augustus	3:00 pm		
SUNDAY			
Leave Fort Augustus	6:30 am	Cycling	8 mph
Leave Fort William	10:30 am	Trail Running	4 mph
Leave shores of Loch Leven	3:30 pm	Kayaking	6 mph
Arrive at Finish Line	4:00 pm		

What was the total distance of the Coast-to-Coast challenge?

1 The height of the giraffe is 5 m. Compare the height of the giraffe with the other items and estimate their heights.

5 m

2 Isla knows that her water bottle can hold two small bottles of apple juice exactly.

She also knows that she needs to fill her water bottle twice to fill a 1 litre bottle.

What is the capacity of the apple juice bottle and Isla's water bottle?

1 litre

3 Nuria knows that one of the small bowls in her kitchen holds about 30 g of cereal. She reckons that the biggest bowl in the cupboard is about three times bigger than the small bowl. How much cereal will the big bowl hold?

⭐ **Challenge**

You will need:

two pieces of A4 paper

five items

Using the two sheets of paper, estimate the area of five items in your environment. One sheet of paper is approximately 30 cm long by 20 cm wide, so has an area of 600 cm² or 0·6 m². Write your estimates in the table below. Then measure the objects you have chosen and calculate the actual area.

Complete the table.

Item	Estimated Area	Actual Area

9.2 Estimating and measuring length

1 Write the length of each bar in centimetres.

a)

```
0  1  2  3  4  5  6  7  8  9  10  11  12  13  14  15
cm
```

b)

```
0  1  2  3  4  5  6  7  8  9  10  11  12  13  14  15
cm
```

c)

```
0  1  2  3  4  5  6  7  8  9  10  11  12  13  14  15
cm
```

d)

```
0  1  2  3  4  5  6  7  8  9  10  11  12  13  14  15
cm
```

e)

```
0  1  2  3  4  5  6  7  8  9  10  11  12  13  14  15
cm
```

f)

```
0  1  2  3  4  5  6  7  8  9  10  11  12  13  14  15
cm
```

2 Estimate the length of each of the bars below, then measure the actual lengths in centimetres and millimetres. Complete the table with your results.

a)

b)

c)

d)

e)

f)

Colour of Bar	Length (cm)	Length (mm)
Green		

3 Amman and Finlay have been discussing whether a person's height is the same as their arm span.

I think the measurements will be different.

I think my height and my arm span will measure the same.

Work with a partner.

- Stand up straight against a wall or door
- Ask your partner to put a piece of masking tape on the wall in line with the top of your head.
- Use a tape measure to measure the distance from the floor to the masking tape.
- Spread your arms out wide.
- With the help of your partner, use a tape measure to measure your arm span to the tips of your fingers.

Are the two measurements identical? Who was correct, Amman or Finlay?
Explain why.

a) Use chalk, a length of string, pieces of scrap paper or masking tape.

Mark your estimates for these lengths:

i) 5 cm   ii) 20 cm   iii) 50 cm   iv) 75 cm   v) 1 m

Now use a ruler, tape measure or a metre stick to measure the lengths accurately and check how close you were.

b) Stride length is the distance covered by two steps. These are the measurements of the stride lengths of animals. Estimate then measure these out using chalk, string, stones or sticks with a measuring tape. Can you stride as far as one of the dinosaurs?

Elephant 200 cm

c)

My stride length is [＿＿＿＿] cm

Triceratops 900 cm

I have to walk [＿＿＿＿＿＿] steps to cover the stride length of a Triceratops.

Brachiosaurus 1872 cm

I have to walk [＿＿＿＿＿＿] steps to cover the stride length of a Brachiosaurus.

1 What is the mass of each object below?

a)

b)

c)

d)

e)

f)

g)

h)

i)

2 Choose six objects from your environment. Estimate the mass of each in grams and then kilograms. Then weigh the objects to find their actual mass. Round your measurements to the nearest half kilogram.

Object	Estimated mass (grams)	Estimated mass (kilograms)	Actual mass (grams)	Actual mass (kilograms)

Can you find objects in your environment that, together, total 5 kg?

One object must have a mass of less than 500 g.

One object must have a mass of between 500 g and 1 kg.

One object must have a mass of more than 1 kg.

Draw your objects and write down how much they weigh in the box below.

9.4 Converting units of length

1 The following measurements have been given in metres. Convert each of the measurements into centimetres.

a)

1·61 m

b)

0·76 m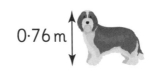

c)

0·96 m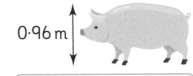

d)

0·57 m

e)

2·87 m

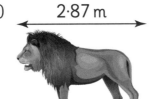

f)

3·19 m

2 The following measurements have been given in centimetres. Convert each of the measurements into millimetres.

a)

5 cm

b)

13 cm

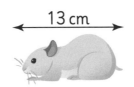

c)

20·4 cm

d)

4·2 cm

e)

 13·5 cm

f)

 63·2 cm

3 a) Complete the following table. The first line has been done for you.

Millimetres (mm)	Centimetres (cm)
20 mm	2 cm
	9 cm
50 mm	
260 mm	
580 mm	
	17 cm

b) Write the rule for changing millimetres to centimetres.

★ **Challenge**

a) Write the objects from Questions 1 and 2 in order from shortest to longest.

b) Find five objects in your environment that would fit *between* two objects in the list. For example, "My own dog is smaller than the dog but taller than the seagull."

9.5 Calculating the perimeter of simple shapes

1 Calculate the perimeter of each of the shapes below.

a)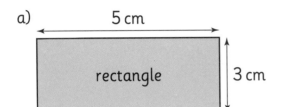

5 cm

3 cm

rectangle

Perimeter = [ ]

b)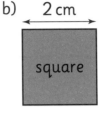

2 cm

square

Perimeter = [ ]

c)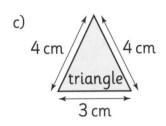

4 cm   4 cm

triangle

3 cm

Perimeter = [ ]

d)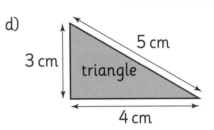

5 cm

3 cm   triangle

4 cm

Perimeter = [ ]

e) 1 cm

rectangle

7 cm

Perimeter = [ ]

f)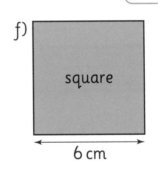

square

6 cm

Perimeter = [ ]

2 a) Use a ruler to take measurements and calculate the perimeter of each shape.
Aim to take the fewest number of measurements to work out each shape's perimeter.
Complete the table.

Square

Hexagon

Rectangle

 Equilateral Triangle

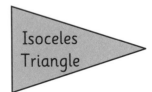 Isoceles Triangle

Shape	Number of measurements I took	Perimeter calculations
Square		
Hexagon		
Rectangle		
Equilateral triangle		
Isosceles triangle		

b) Complete this sentence. The easiest shape to calculate the perimeter of is the

[ ] because [ ]

a) Finlay works out that the perimeter of the rectangle he has just measured is 24 cm. What could the lengths of the sides be?

b) Isla measures the perimeter of a shape. The perimeter is 18 cm. What shape could Isla have been measuring and what would the length of the sides be?

1 Calculate the area of the shapes below in square centimetres (cm²).

a)
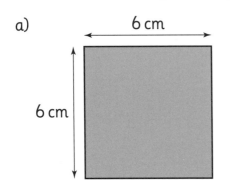
6 cm
6 cm

Area =

b)
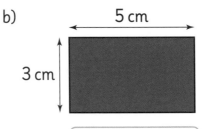
5 cm
3 cm

Area =

c)
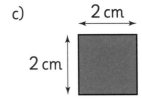
2 cm
2 cm

Area =

2 Use a ruler to measure the shapes below and calculate their area.

Length =

Breadth =

Area =

Length =

Breadth =

Area =

Length =

Breadth =

Area =

3 a) Calculate the area of each of the rooms on the floor plan of this flat.

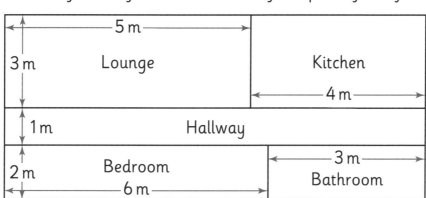

Lounge =

Kitchen =

Hallway =

Bedroom =

Bathroom =

b) What is the total area of the whole flat?

★ **Challenge**

Edinburgh Zoo is creating some new animal enclosures. The area of one must be 36 m².

What possible dimensions could the enclosure have? How many different ways can you find?

9.7 Estimating and measuring capacity

1 What is the volume of these 3D objects?

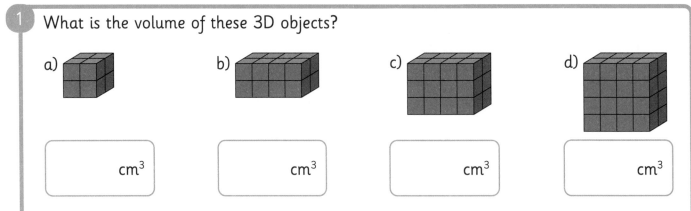

a) ▢ cm³

b) ▢ cm³

c) ▢ cm³

d) ▢ cm³

2 Match the volume of the cubes with the corresponding capacity in millilitres or litres.

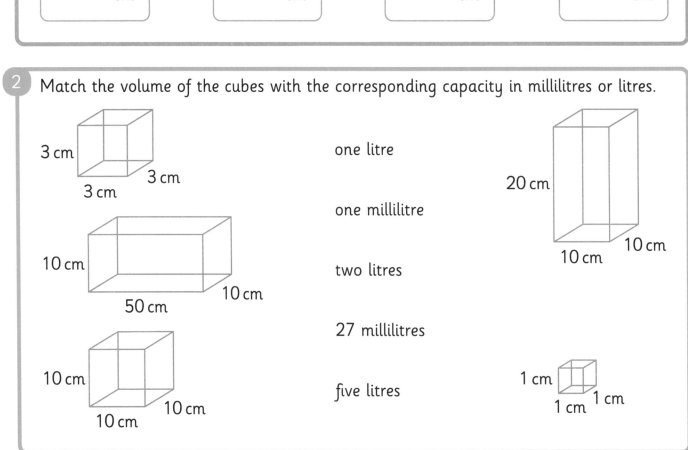

3 cm · 3 cm · 3 cm

one litre

one millilitre

two litres

27 millilitres

five litres

10 cm · 50 cm · 10 cm

10 cm · 10 cm · 10 cm

20 cm · 10 cm · 10 cm

1 cm · 1 cm · 1 cm

3 How much liquid is there in each of the containers below?

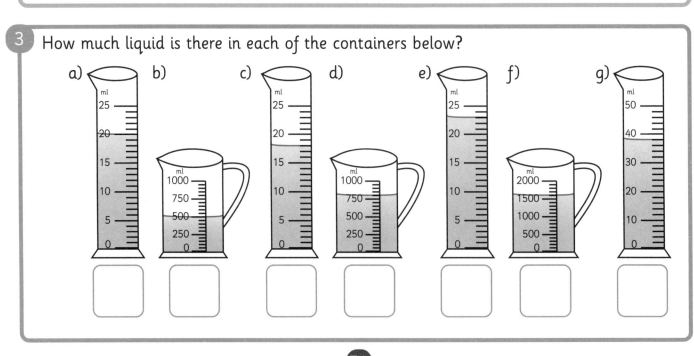

a) ▢ b) ▢ c) ▢ d) ▢ e) ▢ f) ▢ g) ▢

Isla has a small bottle that holds 100 ml. Amman has a larger bottle that holds 700 ml. Neither container has markings on it. Finlay has an empty bucket. Nuria thinks that they can make 100 ml, 200 ml, 300 ml, etc. all the way to 1 litre, by only using the two containers and the empty bucket.

Finlay isn't sure they can. Who is correct? Show your working.

9.8 Finding the volume of cubes and cuboids by counting cubes

1 Match the shapes to the correct calculation to work out the volume in cubic centimetres **and** the actual volume of the shape.

          6 × 1 × 1   18 cm³

          2 × 3 × 3   28 cm³

          2 × 4 × 4   32 cm³

          4 × 3 × 2   6 cm³

          3 × 2 × 2   12 cm³

2 × 5 × 3   24 cm³

2 Sketch a cuboid that has a volume of:

a) 20 cm³

b) 12 cm³

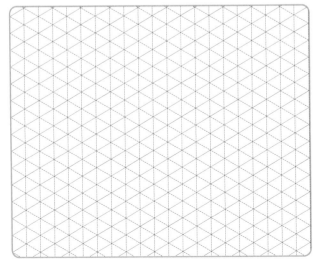

The children have some cubic centimetre blocks. They have been asked to make as many cubes or cuboids as they can using all of their cubes.

Amman	**Isla**	**Finlay**	**Nuria**
	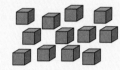	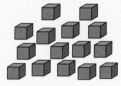	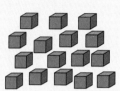

a) Predict who you think will be able to make the most cubes or cuboids. Explain your working.

b) Investigate how many different cubes or cuboids each of the children can make using all of their cubic centimetres. You might want to use blocks or multilink cubes to help you. Complete the table to help you record your answers.

Amman – 9 cubes	
Isla – 12 cubes	
Finlay – 15 cubes	
Nuria – 16 cubes	

1

۱۰	۹	۸	۷	۶	۵	۴	۳	۲	۱
۲۰	۱۹	۱۸	۱۷	۱۶	۱۵	۱۴	۱۳	۱۲	۱۱
۳۰	۲۹	۲۸	۲۷	۲۶	۲۵	۲۴	۲۳	۲۲	۲۱
۴۰	۳۹	۳۸	۳۷	۳۶	۳۵	۳۴	۳۳	۳۲	۳۱
۵۰	۴۹	۴۸	۴۷	۴۶	۴۵	۴۴	۴۳	۴۲	۴۱
۶۰	۵۹	۵۸	۵۷	۵۶	۵۵	۵۴	۵۳	۵۲	۵۱
۷۰	۶۹	۶۸	۶۷	۶۶	۶۵	۶۴	۶۳	۶۲	۶۱
۸۰	۷۹	۷۸	۷۷	۷۶	۷۵	۷۴	۷۳	۷۲	۷۱
۹۰	۸۹	۸۸	۸۷	۸۶	۸۵	۸۴	۸۳	۸۲	۸۱
۱۰۰	۹۹	۹۸	۹۷	۹۶	۹۵	۹۴	۹۳	۹۲	۹۱

What do you notice about the order of this hundred square? Is '1' in the top left square and '100' in the bottom right square? Why do you think this is?

Using the Urdu numbers from the table, write down the corresponding numbers from our decimal number system.

a) ۱۰

b) ۵۰

c) ۱۱

d) ۶۰

e) ۹

f) ۴

g) ۱۰۰

h) ۵۰۰

2 Amman is using a code he made with Urdu numbers to write a message to Finlay. He separates words by using the / symbol.

A	B	C	D	E	F	G	H	I	J	K
۱	۲	۳	۴	۵	۶	۷	۸	۹	۱۰	۱۱

L	M	N	O	P	Q	R	S	T	U	V
۱۲	۱۳	۱۴	۱۵	۱۶	۱۷	۱۸	۱۹	۲۰	۲۱	۲۲

W	X	Y	Z
۲۳	۲۴	۲۵	۲۶

Amman writes this:

۴ ۱۵/ ۲۵ ۱۵ ۲۱/ ۲۳ ۱ ۱۴ ۲۰/۲۰ ۱۵/

۷ ۱۵/ ۲۰ ۱۵ / ۲۰ ۸ ۵/ ۳ ۹ ۱۴ ۵ ۱۳ ۱/

۱۵ ۱۴/ ۶ ۱۸ ۹ ۳ ۱ ۲۵/ ?

What is Amman's message?

[blank answer box]

★ **Challenge**

Let's research Sir David Brewster, a famous Scottish physicist and mathematician.

Research what he is famous for and what impact he has had on the world.

Create a fact file with the information you find. Include the following details:

- His full name, date of birth and when he died.
- Where in Scotland he was from.
- What he was best known for and what he improved.
- Examples of his work (include pictures and diagrams).

11.1 Exploring and extending number sequences

1 Complete the following patterns and sequences:

a)

b)

c)

d)

e) A, C, E, G, I, K, ☐ , ☐ , ☐ , ☐ , ☐

f) A, F, K, ☐ , ☐ , ☐ , ☐ , ☐ , ☐

g) Z, W, T, Q ☐ , ☐ , ☐ , ☐ , ☐

h) ☐ , ☐ , ☐ , M, Q, ☐ , ☐

2 Complete the following number patterns and state the rule:

a) 3, 8, 13, 18, ☐ , ☐ , ☐ .

The rule is ☐ .

b) 2, 4, 8, 16, ☐ , ☐ , ☐ .

The rule is ☐ .

c) 1, 2, 4, 7, 11, ☐ , ☐ , ☐ .

The rule is ☐ .

d) ☐ , ☐ , 92, 84, 76, ☐ , ☐

The rule is ☐ .

An author used the Fibonacci sequence as chapter numbers instead of 1, 2, 3, 4, 5, etc.

What would the next seven chapters be numbered?

Chapter 1	Chapter 2	Chapter 3	Chapter 4	Chapter 5	Chapter 6
Fibonacci chapter 1	Fibonacci chapter 1	Fibonacci chapter 2	Fibonacci chapter 3	Fibonacci chapter 5	Fibonacci chapter

Chapter 7	Chapter 8	Chapter 9	Chapter 10	Chapter 11	Chapter 12
Fibonacci chapter	Fibonacci chapter	Fibonacci chapter	Fibonacci chapter	Fibonacci chapter	Fibonacci chapter

Use the table to help you complete the sequence.

1, 1, 2, 3, 5, ☐ , ☐ , ☐ , ☐ , ☐ , ☐ , ☐ .

1 Are the following expressions true or false? Insert a tick ✓ or cross ✗ to show this.
If **false**, correct them so they are true.

a) $5 \times 4 = 2 \times 9$

b) $3 \times 25 > 80$

c) $1000 + 205 < 2000 - 80$

d) $35 \times 10 \neq 275 + 75$

2 Insert a number or symbol into the star to make the equations complete.

a) $5 \times \; ☆ \; = 49$

b) $78 \; ☆ \; 35 = 43$

c) $56 + \; ☆ \; = 112$

d) $☆ \; - 69 = 54$

e) $100 \; ☆ \; 20 = 5$

f) $☆ \; \div 6 = 12$

3 Read the word problem and complete the number sentences.

a) Amman helped his dad make some biscuits.

They had to put 48 on the baking tray to put in the oven.

Amman could put 12 biscuits in a row on the baking tray.

How many rows were there?

$$12 \times \boxed{} = 48$$

b) Isla collects stickers. She has 57 in her collection.

Her uncle gives her some more and now she has 74.

How many stickers did her uncle give her?

$$57 + \boxed{} = 74$$

c) Amman took some of his biscuits to school.

$$\boxed{} - \boxed{} = 7$$

Everyone in his class got a biscuit. There were 28 children in the class.

He had 7 left. How many biscuits did Amman take to school?

d) Nuria is making some apple pies. She needs 36 apples to make 6 pies.
She only has 24 apples. How many does she need to buy so she has enough?

$$\boxed{} + \boxed{} = \boxed{}$$

★ **Challenge**

Create word problems for the following equations and ask a friend to solve them.
Make sure you know the answers so you can tell them if they're right or wrong!

a) $10 \times \boxed{} = 60$ $\boxed{}$

b) $\boxed{} - 25 = 50$ $\boxed{}$

1 Continue this pattern by drawing the squares and rectangles accurately using a ruler and a protractor.

2 Create a design using 2 cm squares and 2 × 4 cm rectangles. There should be an element of a repeating pattern in your design.

3 Copy this drawing of a house by using a ruler and protractor.

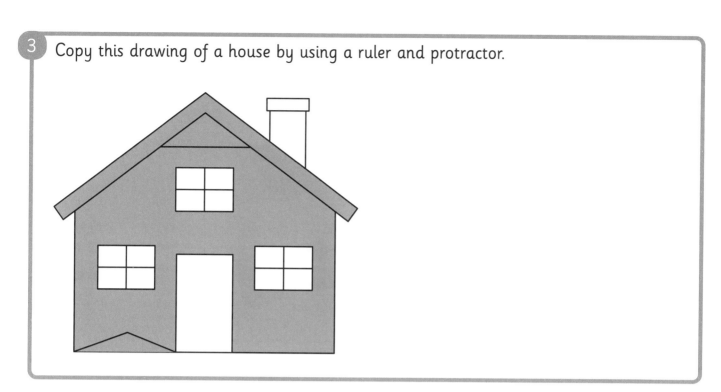

This is the brand logo for Japanese manufacturer Mitsubishi.

It is made up of three diamonds or rhombuses.

Find and draw logos that have the following shapes in them:

- oval
- square
- triangle
- rectangle.

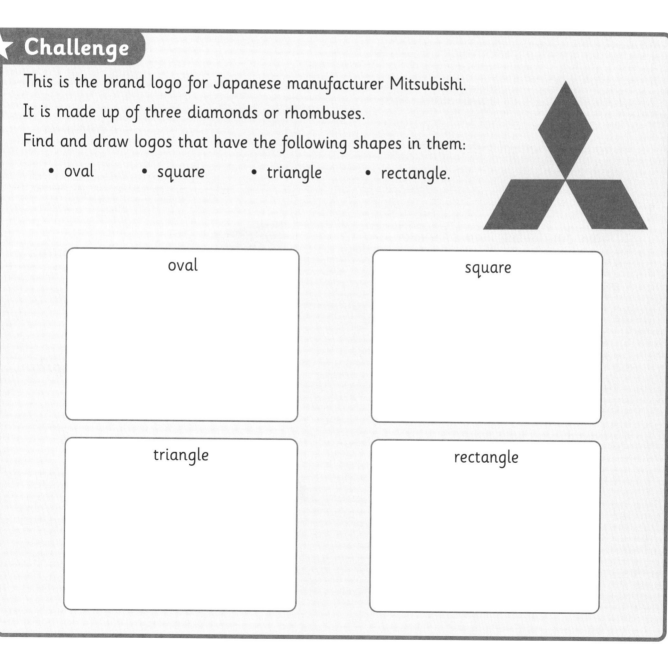

oval	square

triangle	rectangle

1 Match each shape with its name and description.

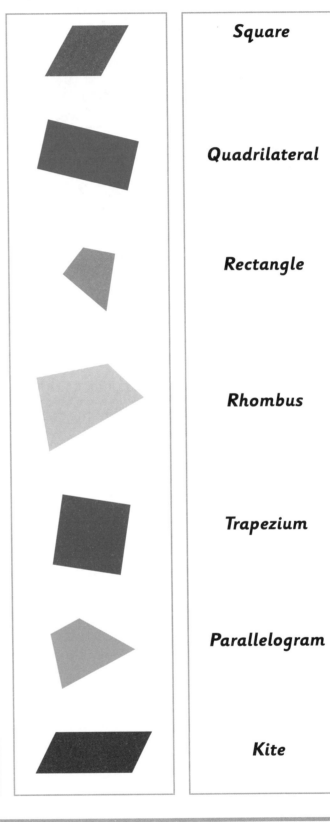

Both pairs of my opposite sides are parallel. I have no right angles.

I have four sides of equal length. My opposite sides are parallel and my opposite angles are equal. I do not have 4 right angles.

Both pairs of my opposite sides are parallel. My opposite sides are equal. I have 4 right angles.

I have 2 pairs of equal sides, that are next to each other. I have one pair of equal sides opposite each other.

I have four sides. Two of these are parallel. My sides might all be different lengths.

I have four equal sides and four equal angles. My angles are all right angles.

I am a shape with 4 sides.

Square

Quadrilateral

Rectangle

Rhombus

Trapezium

Parallelogram

Kite

2 Sort these shapes by writing the letter of the shape into the correct section of the Carroll Diagram.

A   B   C   D   E   F   G   H   I   J

	Exactly four sides	Not a four-sided shape
Has pairs of parallel sides		
No parallel sides		

★ Challenge

Write clues for two of these shapes. There should be at least two clues about its sides and angles for each shape. Ask a friend to guess which shapes you have written the clues for.

A   B   C   D

13.3 Drawing 3D objects

1 Match the 3D object with its top view.

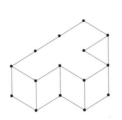 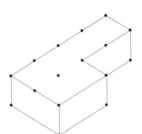 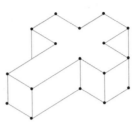 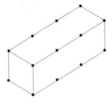

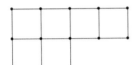 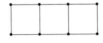 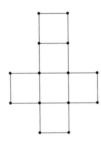 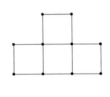

2 On the isometric paper draw:

a) a cube with edges of length 3 cm

b) a 2 cm × 3 cm × 4 cm cuboid

c) a 2 cm × 4 cm × 3 cm cuboid.

3 Complete the table below detailing the top view, side view and end view of the two cuboids you have drawn for Question 2.

	Cuboid b)
Top view	
Side view	
End view	

	Cuboid c)
Top view	
Side view	
End view	

★ Challenge

How many different 3D objects can you make with eight interlocking cubes? Draw two of them on the isometric paper below.

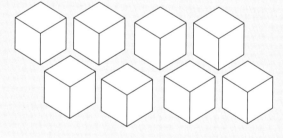

1

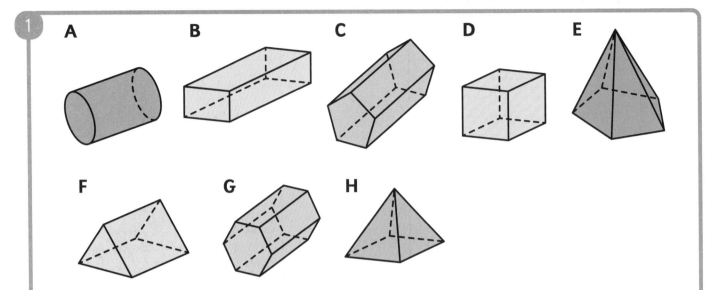

a) Complete the table about the the 3D objects above. Choose a name for each object from these: cylinder, triangular-based pyramid, triangular prism, cube, square-based pyramid, pentagonal prism, pentagonal-based pyramid, hexagonal prism.

	Name of 3D object	Is this a prism? ✓ ✗	Number of faces	Number of edges	Number of vertices
A			3		
	Rectangular prism				
C		✓			
D				12	
E					6
F					
G					
H					

b) Complete this Venn Diagram by writing the letter of the 3D object from A to H in the correct section.

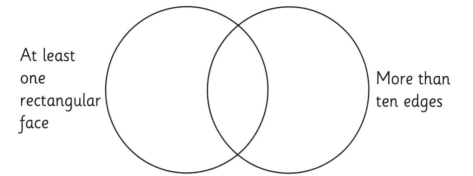

At least one rectangular face

More than ten edges

Write clues to describe two of the 3D objects in this section. There should be at least two clues that refer to the number of faces, edges or vertices. Try to include at least one clue that gives the name of a famous building or structure that is a prism or a pyramid.

Give these to a friend. Can they guess which 3D objects you have described?

1.

2.

14.1 Identifying angles

1   Are these angles **acute**, **right** or **obtuse**? Write the correct word in the answer box.

a)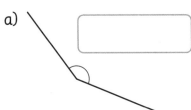

b)

c)

d)

e)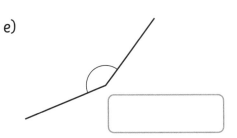

f)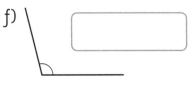

2   Complete the table. Identify the angles as **acute**, **right**, **obtuse** or **straight**.

Letter	Angle
A	
B	
C	
D	
E	
F	
G	
H	
I	
J	

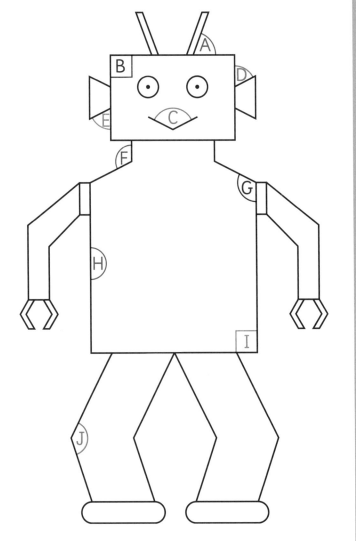

3 An engineer is surveying the land. Label at least one **acute**, one **right**, one **obtuse** and one **straight** angle you can see in the photo.

Draw a picture where there are:

- at least 2 **acute** angles
- at least 4 **obtuse** angles
- at least 3 **right** angles
- at least 5 **straight** angles.

Label the angles you have drawn.

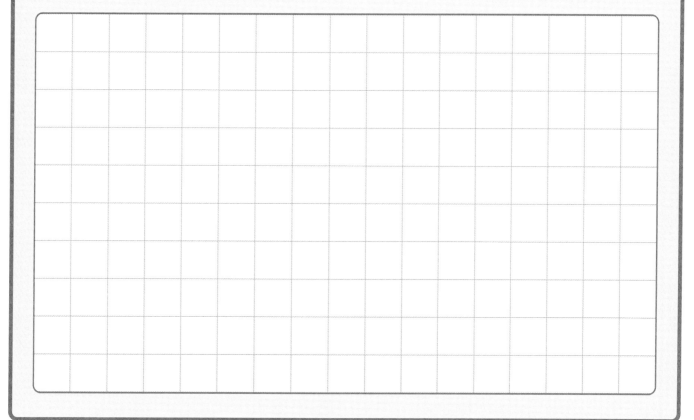

1 Finlay is playing a grid game in the playground with his friends.

Nuria	Mark	Isla
Sheona	Finlay	Mary
Amman	Bill	Karen

N ↑

a) Who is to the:

i) North of Finlay? ☐

ii) South-west of Finlay? ☐

iii) West of Finlay? ☐

iv) North-east of Finlay? ☐

v) South of Finlay? ☐

vi) South-east of Finlay? ☐

vii) East of Finlay? ☐

viii) North-west of Finlay? ☐

b) Complete the following statements:

i) Nuria is ☐ of Finlay.

ii) Karen is ☐ of Mary.

iii) Mark is ☐ of Isla.

iv) Sheona is ☐ of Amman.

2

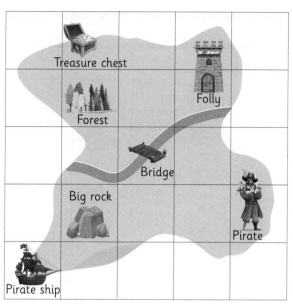

Scurvy McPlunder, the pirate, has returned to Leckie Island to retrieve his hidden treasure. He needs to visit certain landmarks on the island to find the treasure.

Which landmarks does Scurvy travel to, by following these directions?

a) Starting at Scurvy McPlunder (the Pirate), move north-west one square (NW1) then north one square (N1).

b) Now move south-west two squares (SW2).

c) Continue north-east one square (NE1).

d) Finally move north-west one square (NW1).

e) Write directions for Scurvy McPlunder to go from his last landmark to his treasure chest.

1

a) On the grid, plot the following points:

(1, 5) (3, 6) (5, 5) (3, 2)

Join the dots, in order, with straight lines.

What shape have you made?

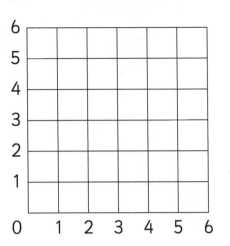

b) On the grid, plot the following points:

(0, 2) (1, 4) (6, 4) (5, 2)

Join the dots, in order, with straight lines.

What shape have you made?

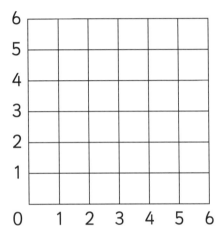

2

a) On the grid, plot the following points and join them up as you go along to make a letter of the alphabet:

(0, 6) (0, 0) (2, 0) (2, 2) (4, 2) (4, 0) (6, 0) (6, 6) (4, 6) (4, 4) (2, 4)

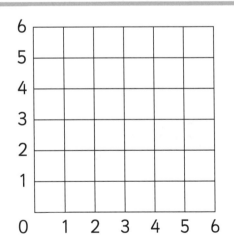

b) Write down the coordinates of the final point needed to complete

the letter.

Draw your initials in capital letters on the grid paper below.

Write down the coordinates needed for a friend to draw your initials.
Write the coordinates in order.

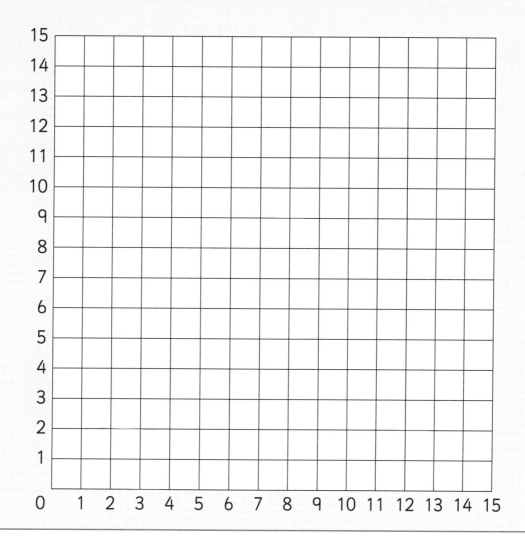

1 In which of these shapes is the dotted line **a line of symmetry**? Write a ✓ or ✗ in the box to show this.

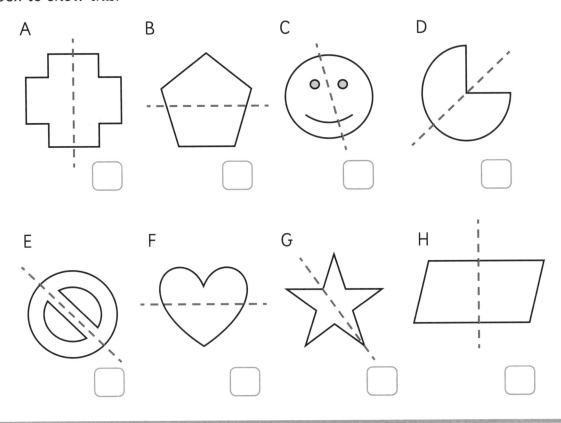

2 a) Is there at least one line of symmetry on each shape? Write a ✓ or ✗ in the box to show this. If you have a mirror, you could use this to check your answers.

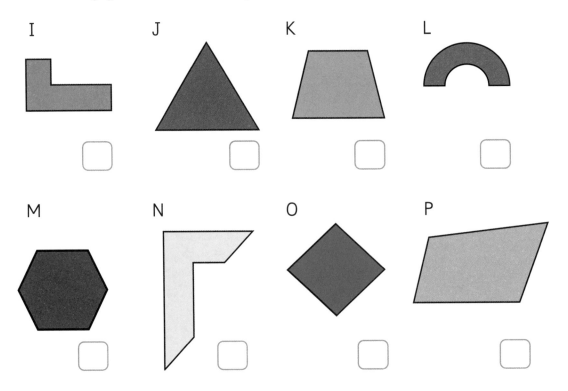

b) Copy and complete the table to sort the shapes.

Has horizontal lines of symmetry	Has vertical lines of symmetry	No lines of symmetry

3 Complete each shape by drawing the reflection in the line of symmetry. If you have a mirror, use it to check.

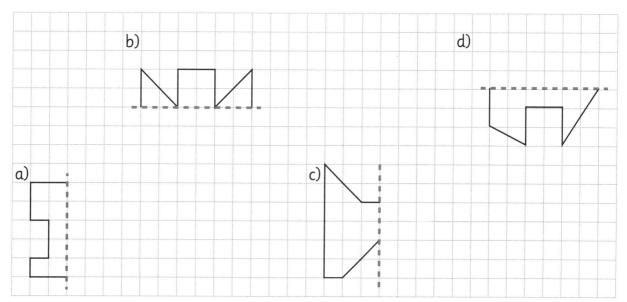

a)

b)

c)

d)

★ Challenge

Draw shapes on the squared paper that have:

a) • one line of symmetry
    • three sides

b) • one line of symmetry
    • eight sides

Show the line of symmetry by drawing a dotted line with a ruler.

1 Complete each pattern by drawing and colouring the reflection. If you have a mirror check your reflected shape.

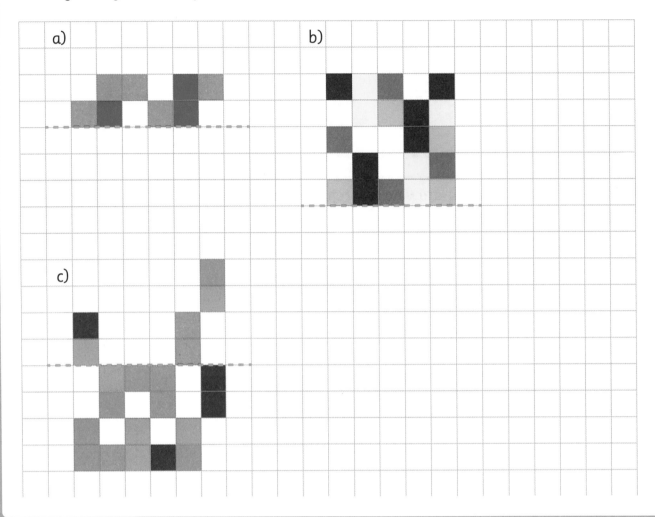

a)

b)

c)

2 Isla and Nuria are creating a design for some artwork. Their design is only half finished. Reflect the pattern to complete their design.

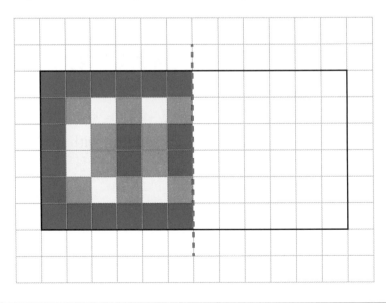

3 Draw another design for Isla and Nuria's artwork. It must be symmetrical and have a vertical line of symmetry. Colour your art design, making sure it is still symmetrical.

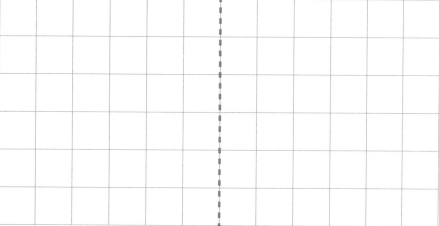

★ **Challenge**

Using exactly four colours, can you colour these rectangles to make four **different** symmetrical designs?

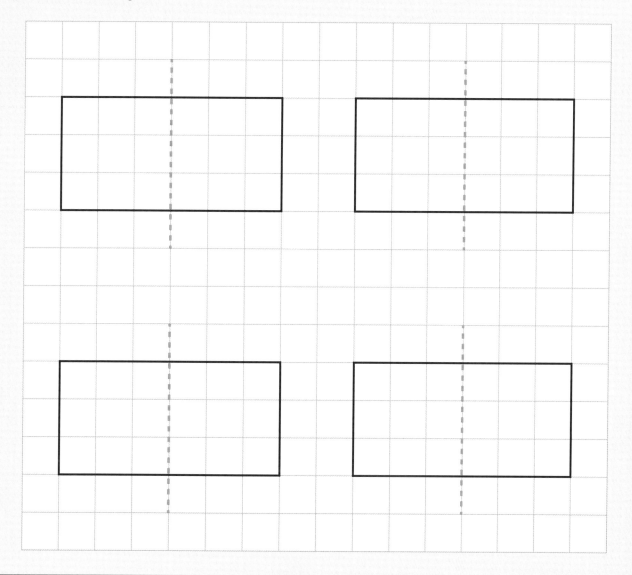

1 We can name the angles in triangles by using the letters on the adjacent sides. For example, the angle at point A in triangle ABC is named **BAC** (you can write it as **BÂC**). Measure the angles in these triangles and record your results in the table.

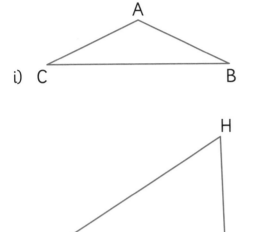

i) C

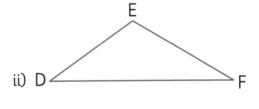

ii) D

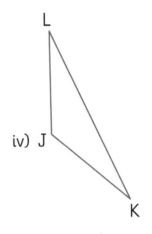

iii) G

iv) J

Name of angle	Angle size
BÂC	130°
AB̂C	
AĈB	

② Use a protractor to measure each angle. Write the size of each angle next to the diagram.

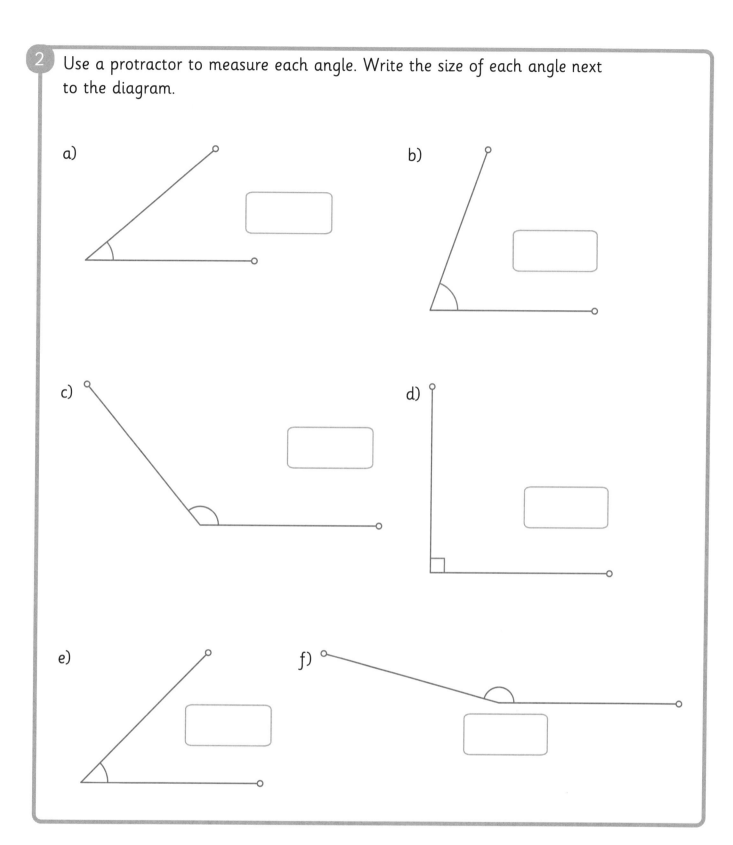

a)

b)

c)

d)

e)

f)

a) What do you notice if you total the three angles in each of the triangles in Question 1?

b) Write possible angles for a new triangle and then draw your triangle using a ruler and protractor. Was your answer correct?

c) Write the possible angles for one more new triangle and then draw it. Do you think you now know the rule for the angles in a triangle? Write your rule.

1 The scale on this map is 1 cm for every 1 km.

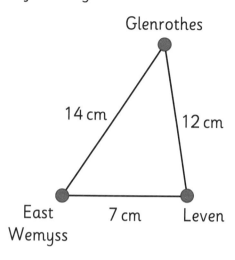

How far is it in real life:

a) from East Wemyss to Leven?

b) from Leven to East Wemyss via Glenrothes?

2 The scale on this map is 1 cm for every 10 miles.

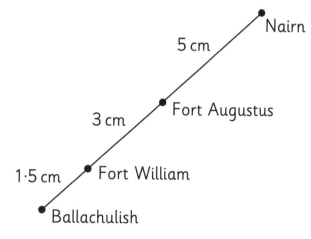

How far is it in real life:

a) from Fort William to Ballachulish?

b) from Fort Augustus to Fort William?

c) from Nairn to Ballachulish?

3 Isla is reading a map of France. The scale is 1 cm for every 40 km.

On Isla's map;

a) Lille is 3 cm from Amiens. What is the actual distance between Lille and Amiens?

b) Dijon is 11 cm from Limoges. What is the actual distance between Dijon and

Limoges?

c) Paris is 8 cm from Dijon, Marseille is 12 cm from Dijon, and Nice is 5 cm from Marseille. If Isla's family are wanting to visit each of these places, what is the

actual distance of this journey?

The scale on this map is 1 cm for every 50 km.

Use a ruler to measure the distances to the nearest centimetre, then answer the questions.

a) Which city is about 150 km south of Inverness?

°Ullapool

Inverness   Aberdeen
                    °

Oban   Dundee
  °   Perth °
Stirling°

Glasgow Edinburgh
   °   °

Dumfries
   °

b) How far is Oban from Glasgow?

c) Amman travelled from Edinburgh to Stirling to Perth and then Dundee with his mum.

How far did they travel?

d) Find two places on the map which are about 200 km away from each other.

1 The bar graph shows the number of people who have different pets. Look at the graph and answer the questions.

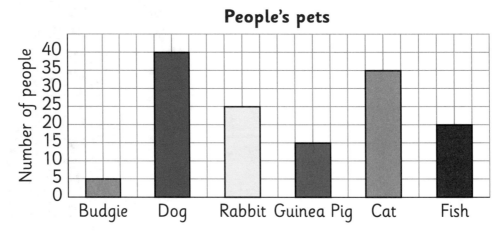

a) How many **more** people had a dog than a rabbit?

b) How many **fewer** people had a guinea pig than a cat?

c) In the survey, which pet got the **lowest** number of votes?

2 Dundee is one of the sunniest cities in Scotland, with an average of 1523 hours of sunshine each year. The pictograph shows the average number of hours of sunshine for the least sunniest six months of the year. Use the graph to answer the questions.

☀ = 10 hours of sunshine

Month	Average number of hours of sunshine
January	☀☀☀☀☀◖
February	☀☀☀☀☀☀☀☀◖
March	☀☀☀☀☀☀☀☀☀☀☀☀
October	☀☀☀☀☀☀☀☀☀◖
November	☀☀☀☀☀☀☀
December	☀☀☀☀☀◖

a) How many more hours of sunshine were there in October compared to December?

b) How many fewer hours of sunshine were there in January compared to November?

c) Which month had the most sunshine?

d) How much sunshine was there in total over these six months?

⭐ Challenge

Nuria has been charting the growth of her Bearded Collie puppy. She has weighed him every five weeks. She wants to answer these two questions:

Question 1 How much did the puppy grow between the ages of 15 weeks and 35 weeks?

Question 2 Between which weigh-ins did the puppy grow the most?

Which question would be easier for her to answer

a) by looking at the graph?

b) by looking at the table? Explain your thinking.

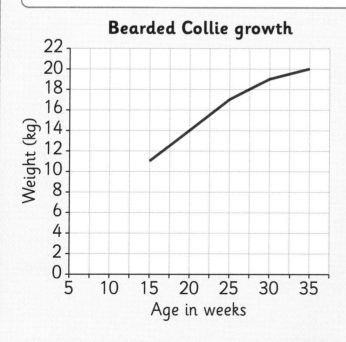

Bearded Collie growth

Bearded Collie growth	
Age in weeks	Weight (kg)
15	11
20	14
25	17
30	19
35	20

1 Isla's class are deciding what to continue selling at their school tuck shop. They decide to poll the pupils to in the school to find out which snacks are most popular.

Snack	Tally	Frequency
Cheese and ham cups	卌 卌 卌 卌 卌 |||	
Melon slices	卌 卌 卌 卌 卌 卌 卌		
Fruit smoothies	卌 卌 卌 卌	
Porridge	卌 卌 卌 卌 卌 卌 ||	
Crisps	卌 卌 卌 卌 ||||	
Veg sticks	卌 卌 卌		

a) Complete the Frequency column of the table.

b) How many children like porridge as a snack from the tuck shop?

c) How many children like snacks with fruit or vegetables?

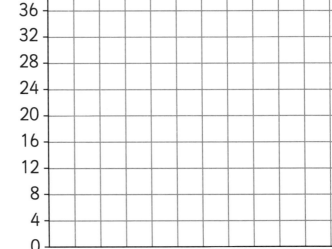

d) How many more children like cheese and ham cups than crisps?

e) Display the data in the table as a bar graph. Label the axes. Remember to give your graph a suitable title!

Find out what pets the children in your class have by conducting your own survey.

Before you start, you might want to decide which pets you want to include.

Create a frequency table of your results.

Display your data as a bar graph. Choose an appropriate scale for your axes and label them. Give your graph a suitable title.

Type of pet	Tally	Frequency

1   The school tuck shop is gathering information about the flavours of crisps they sell in a month. The data is displayed in this pie chart.

Salt & Vinegar	40
Ready salted	20
Cheese & Onion	20
Prawn Cocktail	10

Salt & Vinegar

Ready salted

Cheese & Onion

Prawn Cocktail

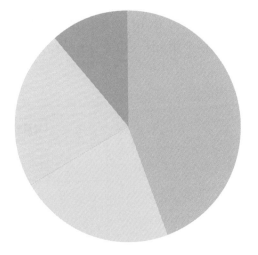

a) Using the information in the table, write the correct crisp flavour in the correct part of the pie chart.

b) How many **more** people bought Salt and Vinegar than Prawn Cocktail?

c) Which flavour of crisps sold the **least** at the tuck shop?

d) How many crisps were sold in the month?

2   This pie chart shows the favourite cities to visit of 48 parents in Finlay's class.

Favourite City

a) What was the most popular city?

b) How many adults chose:

i)   Aberdeen?

ii) Dundee?

iii) Edinburgh?

iv) Glasgow?

Aberdeen

Edinburgh

Glasgow

Dundee

Follow the steps given to complete this pie chart.

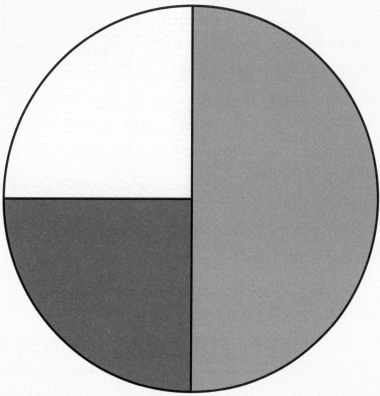

a) Write down a question you could ask and three possible answers.

b) How many people could you survey?

Which numbers could be halved or quartered to create the above pie chart? Write them down.

c) Label the pie chart, including how many people each section represents.

15.4 Collecting data

1 The children have written these 'big questions'. What types of data will they collect for their questions? Complete the table by writing the letter of each question in the correct column.

Category Data (Words)	Category Data (Numbers)	Time Series Data

a) I wonder how many trains run from Edinburgh to Glasgow during the week?

b) I wonder what people in our class want to work as when they are older?

c) I wonder how many different places people have lived over the course of their lives?

d) I wonder what the most popular ice-cream flavour is?

e) I wonder how long it takes for a can of fizzy juice to lose its fizz?

f) I wonder how many kilometres we each walk in a day at school?

2 Match each inquiry to the correct type of graph to show the data. You can match more than one inquiry to the same graph.

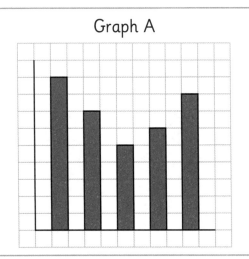

Graph A

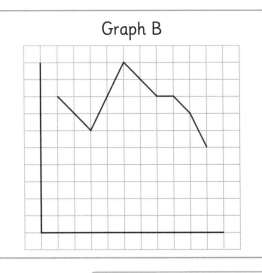

Graph B

a) I wonder how many mobile phones are sold each day?

b) I wonder how the types of flowers differs between different areas?

c) I wonder what is the most popular place to go on holiday?

d) I wonder how much rain falls in my hometown?

a) Write a big question that you would need to collect category data (numbers) for.

b) Write a big question that you would need to collect category data (words) for.

c) Write a big question that you would need to collect time series data for.

d) Go online (ask permission first) and find out which companies collect the most data. Find out what kind of data they collect, how they collect the data and how they use this data. Who do they share this data with?

16.1 Predicting and explaining simple chance situations

1   Use the probability scale to help you to complete the table.

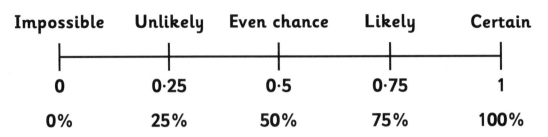

Impossible	Unlikely	Even chance	Likely	Certain
0	0·25	0·5	0·75	1
0%	25%	50%	75%	100%

Event	Probability	Explanation
Saturday will come after Friday.		
I was younger last week.		
I will have 12 friends at my birthday party.		
If I roll a dice three times, I will roll a 6 all three times.		
If I had 1–10 number tiles in a bag and reached in, I will pull out an even number.		
If I had 1–10 number tiles in a bag and reached in, I will pull out a number 11.		

2   You have six green, three blue, two red and one yellow cubes in a bag.

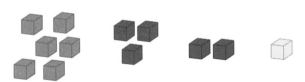

a) What is the probability of drawing a blue cube?

b) What is the probability of drawing a green cube?

c) What is the probability of drawing a pink cube?

d) Do you have a greater or less chance of drawing a blue cube than a green cube? Why?

e) What colour of cube do you have the least chance of pulling from the bag? Why?

3 Collect a ball or scrunch up a piece of paper into a ball shape. Collect a bin or some kind of tub to throw the ball into.

a) Predict how many times you think you will be able to get the ball in the bin if you throw it 10 times.

b) What would the probability of this be?

c) Test this out! Throw the ball into the bin 10 times. Record your results in the chart below. Use a ✔ if the ball goes in the bin, record an ✗ if it doesn't.

d) What was your accuracy?

e) Do your results match your prediction?

f) What is your revised probability of getting the ball in the bin?

g) Will your probability of getting the ball in the bin increase or decrease if you stand further away?

a) Which spinner would you choose if you wanted to increase your chance of landing on:

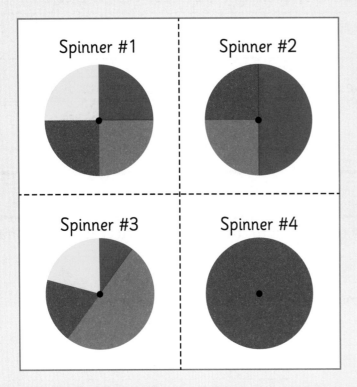

- Blue

- Red

- Green

- Yellow

b) Draw your own spinners to maximise the chance of landing on each colour.

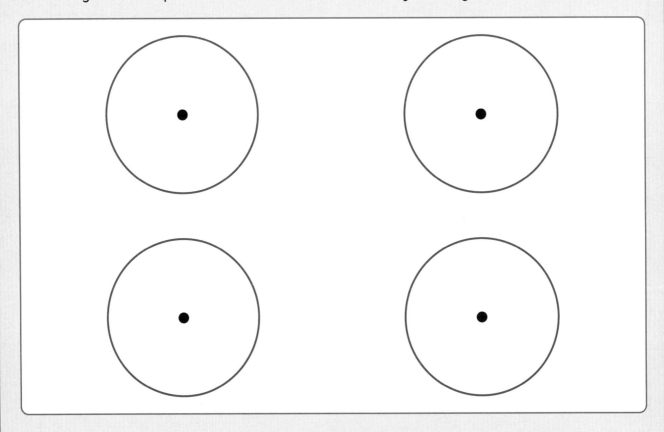